clarity
how to accomplish
what matters most

Ann Daly, PhD

Wollemi Pine Press 2007

Copyright © 2007 by Ann Daly

ISBN 978-0-9797295-0-8

Designed by Angela Rodgers

Printed on demand by lulu.com

Published by Wollemi Pine Press
PO Box 4216
Austin, TX 78765
512/454-0531
wollemi@anndaly.com

"It's beautiful and simple and right on.
Just the experience of dancing through
this visually graceful book dissipates the fog."

clarity
how to accomplish
what matters most

"A practical, creative guide for living every day
the way you really want to. Wise and delightful."

Also by Ann Daly

Done into Dance: Isadora Duncan in America

Critical Gestures: Writings on Dance and Culture

When Writing Becomes Gesture

in memory of my father,

Edwin R. Daly

More important than the quest
for certainty
is the quest for clarity.

François Gautier

contents

2   introduction

32   press pause

50   pay attention

66   ask questions

82   ask more questions

102   write it down

121   acknowledgments

on a clear day you can see the forest **and** the trees

When I am experiencing clarity, I can hear all the notes of every instrument in a musical arrangement. I can spout out wonderfully witty statements, and I can pound out exact, concise sentences. I can whip up a three-course meal with everything 'cooking' at the same time.

We've all had the experience.

Remember?

It was a time when life, or work, seemed to
flow effortlessly. You knew what you wanted,
and how to make it happen. You enjoyed each
step of the way, and you loved the results. No
stress, no struggle, no neurotic procrastination.

A friend of mine, a university professor,
describes clarity as a sense of

one with all.

The trick is to make every day a clear day.

When I hear the word **clarity**,

I think of focused behavior,

purposeful intent, and

almost can't-help-yourself energy.

JULIA solar energy activist

I know it
when I see it

How to define clarity?

It has no form or substance of its own. Rather, we recognize it by what it lacks: obstruction, defect, interference, ambiguity...

Our best understanding of clarity doesn't come from the dictionary. We discover it in metaphor.

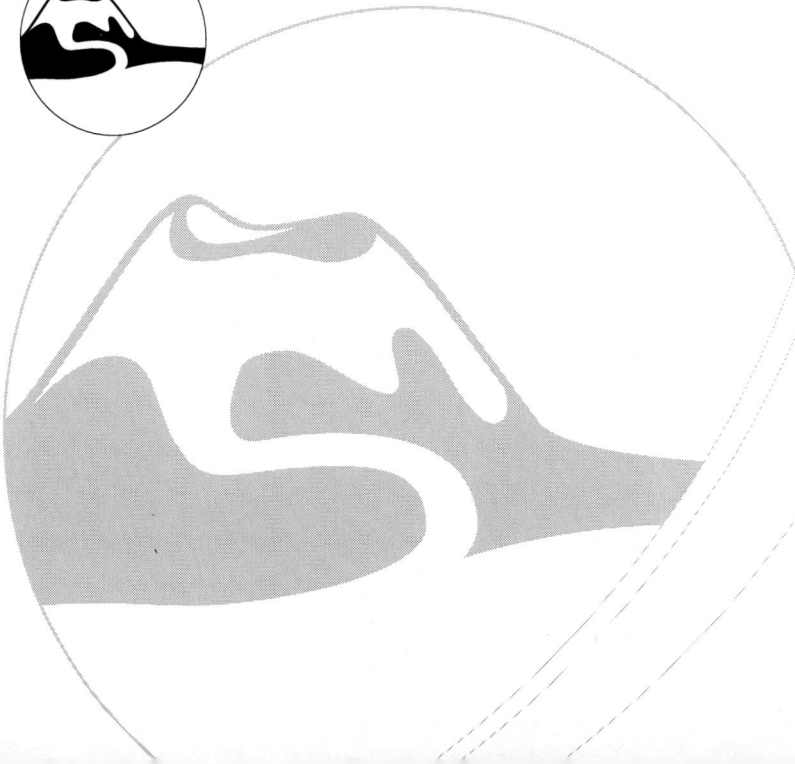

beauty

For me the greatest beauty always lies
in the greatest clarity.

GOTTHOLD EPHRAIM LESSING

communication

purity

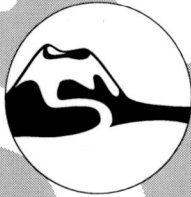

I see a small stream that was tucked away up in the Jemez Mountains in New Mexico, where my dad used to take me fishing when I was a boy. I can still feel the cold on my skin, hear the wind blowing through the massive pine trees, and the gentle splashing of the water.

SIMON business consultant

When I have clarity, I feel most myself.

GLORIA educator

Clarity is knowing who I am and how I am best expressed in the world. Clarity is an internal **yes.**

YVETTE visual artist

If I'm not clear, I'm not being me.

MARGARET administrator

When I worry about something, I am constantly looking at all the points of entry. When I find clarity, there is but one point of entry, and that is me.

LEILAH executive director

clarity
returns us
to ourselves

Clarity is a psychic space where we can live,
work, and love with the most authenticity
and the least effort. For Andrea, director of
her own dance company, being clear keeps
her connected with her unique artistic vision.
Whatever your vision, practicing clarity
grounds you there, at the source of well-being
and self-confidence.

clarity is mission critical

When life is out of whack, when the demands are overwhelming, when you're not feeling your best, clarity keeps you focused on what matters most. It refuses the distractions and the obstacles. It prevents us from yielding to the daily temptation to live "in the thick of thin things" (Stephen R. Covey).

Clarity is a process of revealing what we already know but tend to forget in the morass of everyday life. It reminds us what matters most.

In organizational parlance, clarity guards against "mission creep." Because when we opt-in to too many opportunities, chase too many challenges, or please too many people, we accomplish less, rather than more.

We get distracted by the fact that we can do something, says Sam, who designs websites, **even if it's not part of our original goal/agenda/mission.** His mantra, borrowed from the civil rights movement: **keep your eyes on the prize.**

For further reading

The Seven Habits of Highly Effective People
Stephen R. Covey

Necessary Dreams
Anna Fels

Presence: Human Purpose and the Field of the Future
Betty Sue Flowers et al.

Man's Search for Meaning
Victor E. Frankl

The Soul in the Computer
Barbara Waugh

high road or
low road, clarity
will lead you
in the right
direction

A sense of purpose, says Yvette, **a visual artist, needs a sense of direction.**

Gary (he's a research engineer) puts it this way: **Clarity is found at the junction between knowing and not knowing. It is from that junction that you can take off in a new direction.**

The route may not be MapQuest precise, but you know where you're headed. You set out confidently, deftly navigating the unexpected byways and detours.

A matter that becomes clear

ceases to concern us.

NIETZSCHE

The quickest way to a **solution** is through clarity

I am the daughter of an engineer. I was raised on file folders, and one of my most vivid childhood memories is the click-click-click of my father's plastic rotary labelmaker.

At retirement, my father became ghastly thin and weak. You can see in the photos of the party we threw him, he looks more like a corpse than a man.

After a year of tests, the doctors threw up their hands and pronounced him "depressed." We were disbelieving, but there wasn't anything to be done.

A problem clearly stated is a problem half-solved.

DOROTHEA BRANDE

The phone call finally came. I took it in the living room, standing by the old steamer trunk, listening to my father report the news. A kidney tumor.

"What a relief!" I blurted out. As I heard the words hit the air, I tried to snatch them back.

"No, no, Anna," he reassured me. "You're absolutely right. The first step is defining the problem. Now we can find the solution."

Countless times I had heard him say those words, but never were they so compelling.

You've got to **accentuate** the clarity & minimize uncertainty

When you're clear, you can sort things out calmly, even playfully. Decision-making becomes easier. No wheel-spinning, no angsting.

Even more, clarity helps you to:

REMAIN CALM

SET PRIORITIES

PLAN ACTION

CONTROL TIME

SUSTAIN MOMENTUM

ACHIEVE GOALS

Clarity is all about
how I choose to spend
my available time.
LINDA arts administrator

In Chekhov's "Three Sisters," Olga, Masha, and Irina feel stuck in their small provincial town. At every opportunity they voice their desire to go "to Moscow!"

"Only to go to Moscow! I beg you, let us go! There's nothing on earth better than Moscow! Let us go, Olga! Let us go!"

But by the end of the play, they are further away than ever from the life of their dreams.

Are we **there** yet?

Why do some people make it "to Moscow!" while others just keep repeating the refrain?

In order to change, in order to achieve, in order to live the dream, we need to do more than speak the words. We need to take action.

Clarity is the catalyst to action, because with clarity comes commitment. When you're committed, action takes surprisingly little effort.

clarity))) commitment))) action

What stands in the way of clarity?

internal chatter

people-pleasing

anxiety

self-doubt

fear

deadlines

indecision

illness

exhaustion

denial

stress

obsession

information overload

chores

workaholism

television

perfectionism

drugs & alcohol

ego

procrastination

second-guessing

escapism

What are your
top 3 roadblocks to clarity?

limiting beliefs

self-censorship

mixed emotions

depression

insecurity

anger

interruptions

over-commitment

resistance

bad habits

frustration

1
_____

2
_____

3
_____

⚡⚡⚡⚡⚡⚡

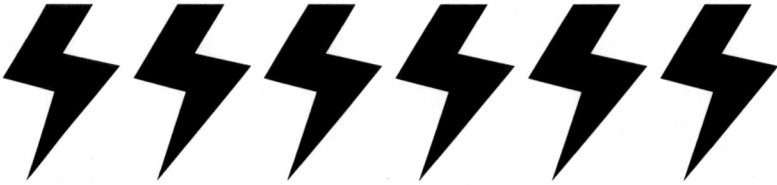

don't wait for **lightning** to strike

Clarity comes when invited.

ANN composer

In the movie "Network," Howard Beale ("the mad prophet of the airwaves") describes his voice-out-of-the-darkness visitation as a "cleansing moment of clarity."

In the Bible, Saul converts after encountering a blinding light on the road to Damascus.

In the comics, a character has her "aha" moment when the proverbial light bulb appears aloft and aglow.

But in everyday life, how often does lightning strike? How often do we "see the light"? How often do we experience an epiphany?

Not often enough.

So instead of waiting for clarity to descend from the skies, create it for yourself.

good news,
bad news

things being in focus

everything is visible

to the point of transparency

a gut feeling of knowing

no questions about it

in tune

in the flow

MILOS choreographer

I've already broken the bad news. You cannot count on clarity to strike in your hour of need. Because clarity is not a magical moment. It's not an outcome. Clarity is a process. It is a habit of mind.

Now for the good news.

THIS IS A HABIT OF MIND YOU CAN LEARN.

What follows is a five-step process that will keep you thinking clearly and acting purposefully.

You can use this process to work out a particular issue, and you can use this process to change your whole approach to life. Either way, it will give you a way to get clear, and get going.

press Pause

the pause that
refreshes

Once upon a time, the machines that delivered our music came with buttons rather than a wheel.

These were mechanical buttons, whose activation required a direct and deliberate press of the finger, akin to a manual typewriter.

When you wanted to take a break, you pressed the PAUSE button. This didn't portend a dramatic exit, just a breather. An interlude. A rest stop.

Pressing PAUSE is the first step to the habit of clarity. You've got to take a direct and deliberate time-out. Every day. For fifteen minutes.

sit back, relax, and do **nothing**

The truth is, if everyone committed to 15 minutes of nothing a day, there would likely be no coaching industry. Because if everyone committed to 15 minutes of nothing a day, they would likely understand the complexities of their desires and fears intimately enough to navigate them without a coach.

Instead, we run around doing too much for too little payoff. We have become a culture of "multi-taskers." But the research is in, and it's conclusive: doing more than one thing at a time earns diminished returns.

If you're moving too quickly, the passing view is blurry. You'll never find, let alone maintain, clarity.

Doing nothing permits us to relax into ourselves. (It's like my first pilates teacher used to say, as we were struggling so hard to simply locate those elusive core muscles: "More feeling, less effort.") We have space to

Follow effective action with quiet reflection.
From the quiet reflection will come even more
effective action.

PETER F. DRUCKER

notice what thoughts and emotions rise to the top. Our more risky or resistant feelings have space to make themselves known. Back burner ideas are given a fighting chance to make it to the front burner.

Pressing PAUSE is a daily check-in. It implicitly asks what former New York City Mayor Ed Koch repeatedly inquired of his constituents: "How am I doing?"

It's not an end in itself, though. Fifteen minutes of nothing a day is the foundation for doing the work of the other four steps. Musically speaking, it keeps the necessary beat, so that rhythm, melody, and harmony can complete the composition.

But I must warn you: once you break past the initial discomfort, 15 minutes of nothing a day is highly addictive.

seek,
stand **still,**
and you will find

I spent long days and nights in the studio seeking
that dance which might be the divine expression
of the human spirit through the medium of the
body's movement. For hours I would stand quite
still, my two hands folded between my breasts,
covering the solar plexus. My mother often
became alarmed to see me remain for such long
intervals quite motionless as if in a trance—but
I was seeking and finally discovered the central
spring of all movement, the crater of motor
power, the unity from which all diversities of
movements are born.

Modern dance pioneer Isadora Duncan invented an entirely new vocabulary for dance at the turn of the 20th century. Nearly single-handedly, she transformed what was considered a lowly form of entertainment into a high art.

Duncan forged this new vocabulary after years spent absorbing the lessons of visual art, music, science, philosophy, and literature. But it wasn't until she secluded herself in her Paris studio that she distilled these ideas into a physical language.

In her memoir, *My Life*, Duncan describes this artistic turning point.

Don't be fooled by the purple prose. Duncan was not channeling the gods of the dance. She was giving herself the space and time—after several long years building the foundation of a legendary career in San Francisco, Chicago, New York, London, Paris—to literally listen to her body. And the rest, as they say, is history.

It is in our idleness,
in our dreams,
that the

submerged

truth

sometimes
comes
to the top.

VIRGINIA WOOLF

the first **step**
is the hardest

For some of my coaching clients, 15 minutes of nothing a day is their first homework assignment. The outcome tells me a lot about a new client.

For many (most?) of us, the prospect of 15 minutes of nothing is unappealing, uncomfortable, and unachievable.

Giving up our habitual distractions is like quitting coffee. Withdrawal gives us the jitters. Initially it feels downright unbearable.

We're also afraid of what's going to come up when we slow down. Stuff we want to leave in the past. Stuff we'd rather not deal with. Stuff we're tired of dealing with. Stuff we're afraid to let glimpse the light of day.

But fear is not a signal to retreat, writes Susan Jeffers in *Feel the Fear and Do It Anyway*. Fear is "a green light to move ahead."

Ask yourself

What are the 3 worst things that could possibly happen if I spend time listening to myself?

1 _____

2 _____

3 _____

How would I handle them?

1 _____

2 _____

3 _____

I find that starting the day right is a major assist to assure that the days will be clear. A "look and listen" walk helps me to connect with the world outside my head.

KAREN professor

Movement can return me to clarity. Just walking outside and watching birds, playing with my dogs, weeding, or mowing will loosen the hold of distractions. Deliberately dancing like an idiot, enjoying the motion of my body, laughing at the jiggles in my middle-aged body will do the same thing.

BARBARA sculptor

When I am searching for clarity, I head for nature. For me, it is the mountains, for the sights, sounds, smells, and textures.

LOU business consultant

I get outside, change my view a bit, take a walk, dig in my garden, hug my family, smell fresh air, enjoy a cup of tea, or just take a break.

LINDA arts administrator

The swimming pool is a place where I lose track of time momentarily. I stop thinking, and I can see things in a new way.

GARY research engineer

climb into a hammock

lay in corpse pose

soak in the tub

walk around the neighborhood

sit in the garden

Brainstorm 3 ways
that you can do nothing

1 _____

2 _____

3 _____

how to do nothing

First, rule out anything that is goal-oriented, even weeding and exercise. Although it may seem mindless, any goal monopolizes your attention.

Second, don't get too comfortable. Dozing withdraws your attention, rather than heightening your awareness.

Third, don't fight the initial antsiness you may feel, or the boredom. Just stay with it, and it will subside.

Fourth, if you become preoccupied with measuring your 15 minutes, set an egg timer to keep track of time for you.

Fifth, locate yourself in a time and space when and where you won't be interrupted by phones, family, clients, etc.

Sixth, think in terms of change from your usual routine. Move to a calm environment, slow your speed, deepen your breath, shift from precise focus to general awareness.

if it ain't **scheduled,**
it ain't gonna happen

Use this empty schedule to locate the 15 minutes
of every day when you will do nothing

	Mon	Tues	Wed	
6				
7				
8				
9				
10				
11				
12				
1				
2				
3				
4				
5				
6				
7				
8				
9				
10				
11				
12				

Thurs	Fri	Sat	Sun

pay
Attention

2

and now things get **curiouser** and curiouser

Take your inspiration from these world-class observers

Sherlock Holmes

Galileo

Margaret Mead

Alexis de Tocqueville

Sigmund Freud

Jane Goodall

Oliver Sacks

Dorothea Lange

I pressed a sign onto my refrigerator door a number of years ago. It's a slim horizontal magnet, colorfully decorated, that always reminds me: "It comes from taking notice."

CLARITY COMES FROM TAKING NOTICE.

Once you've mastered 15 minutes of nothing a day, you're present and primed for active listening. To yourself. What can you observe about your own thinking patterns, emotional themes, and behavioral habits? This personal profiling is essential to the five-step process, because it is the basic material that will either block or enable the flow of clarity.

I'm not talking about turning into a narcissist, gazing admiringly at yourself in every passing mirror. I'm just talking about getting curious.

Curiosity is the thirst of the soul.

SAMUEL JOHNSON

check your **judgment** at the door

There is, of course, a catch. In order for your observations to be useful, you must suspend all judgment.

AND YOU THOUGHT 15 MINUTES OF NOTHING WAS A STRETCH.

Clear thinking requires that we understand the distinctions among the perceptual processes of observing, analyzing, interpreting, and judging, even though they are interwoven in our everyday lives, enabling us to make sense of the world. More often than not, we slip-slide unconsciously among the four processes. In general, our culture is very quick to jump directly from observation to judgment.

I remember once when I was driving with a date in his truck. I have always owned compact cars, so being perched up high above the madding crowd was a great novelty for me. I verbalized this sense of minor wonder, only to be met with defensiveness. He interpreted my observation as a judgment, and a negative judgment at that.

Judgment shut down that conversation, just as judgment shuts down the process of observation.

As you pay attention to your thoughts, emotions, and actions, it's important to keep the impulsive rush to judgment in check. Can you remember what it was like as a kid, when feeling wonder was fun enough? Can you watch yourself with that same wonder, at a slight distance, without letting personal baggage cloud your vision? Can you skip the color commentary?

Can you play the role of anthropologist, eager to study yourself as the most fascinating subject around?

OBSERVATION **what does it look like?**

ANALYSIS **how does it work?**

INTERPRETATION **what does it mean?**

JUDGMENT **does it succeed?**

You can observe a lot just by watching.
YOGI BERRA

Think, dear sir, of the world you carry within you,
and call this thinking what you will; whether it be
remembering your own childhood or yearning
toward your own future—

only be attentive
to that which rises up

in you

and set it

above everything

that you observe

about you.

What goes on in your innermost being

is worthy of your whole love.

RAINER MARIA RILKE

how to
pay attention

I like to watch.

CHANCE in Jerzy Kosinski's *Being There*

As you pay more attention to yourself, you'll discover two different kinds of awareness. One is global awareness, and the other is detailed awareness.

Global awareness takes in the overall scene. It's like focusing a camera. You're attuning to yourself in an open, general, relaxed way. It leads to a "hmmm."

Detailed awareness focuses on a single component of the big picture. It's like using a zoom-lens camera. You're using intense concentration to reveal a deeper layer of information. It leads to an "aha!"

Detailed awareness requires a level of energy that no one can sustain for long. And you wouldn't want to anyway, because you'd be losing the forest for the trees.

What you want to develop, instead, is a technique that alternates between global and detailed awareness.

For example, if global awareness reveals a need to be right, spend the next week focusing on the words or bodily sensations that come up when you're feeling the itch to win your point. Then return to global awareness, given what you learned, to gain even more insight into what's happening.

Conscious self-awareness brings you one step closer to living with clarity, because it's usually our own stuff—the stuff that we ignore, or resist, or resent—that gets in the way.

To see clearly is

poetry, prophecy,

& religion—
all in one.

JOHN RUSKIN

the story of Marla, a **perfectionist**

Marla was a classic overachiever. She was a successful arts scholar and practitioner whose tenure as a professor was a sure thing, as long as she finished her book on time. She came to me for coaching, worried that she would miss her looming deadline.

It became apparent, and Marla was the first one to point out, that she was a perfectionist. Her hyper-developed critical skills made her a brilliant scholar, but as an approach to life and work, it was paralyzing her.

Marla recognized intellectually that this perfectionism was derailing her book, but she didn't understand enough about the perfectionism to change it. Besides, in some important respects, perfectionism had served her too well for too long to just abandon it.

So I asked Marla to pay attention. I asked her to spend the week before our next session simply taking notice when she was telling herself she "should" do something. I gave her strict instructions.

Don't analyze it, interpret it, or judge it. Don't try to intervene in any way. Just notice it.

The next week, Marla reported in. She told me that when a "should" surfaced, it was followed by, "I don't wanna, and it's okay." For her that was an equally powerful—but previously ignored—message, and it supplied her with an opening to move through this major blockage.

it takes
practice
practice
practice

Conscious self-awareness begins awkwardly, with calculated effort, but with practice it becomes second nature.

To begin, CHOOSE ONE THING (a thought, emotion, or action) from the list of clarity roadblocks you wrote in the introductory chapter (page 27).

Spend a week paying attention to that one thing—curiously, dispassionately, lovingly. Study it as if you were a botanist gathering information about an extraordinarily beautiful new species.

Take notice of

what it feels or looks like

what it reminds you of

when it occurs

what precedes or triggers it

how it begins

what it is connected to
or accompanied by

whether it has a repeated
trajectory or sequence

how long it lasts

how intense it is

how it dissipates or ends

ask
Questions

one question
is **worth**
a thousand answers

Step three arrives without fanfare, because, as you will discover, curiosity slides right into questioning. Once you have become present to yourself by pressing pause and paying attention, you will find yourself naturally wondering "How... ?" and "What... ?"

That's when you realize it.

CLARITY IS AN INQUIRY.

Questions drive this self-inquiry. They provide depth, and detail. They connect the dots. They reveal what's been ignored, lost, or forgotten. They dislodge whatever's stuck. They cut through the clutter and debris. They dissolve the waxy buildup.

Keep asking those questions, and your priorities will become increasingly transparent— and powerful. No more feeling confused or conflicted about what matters most.

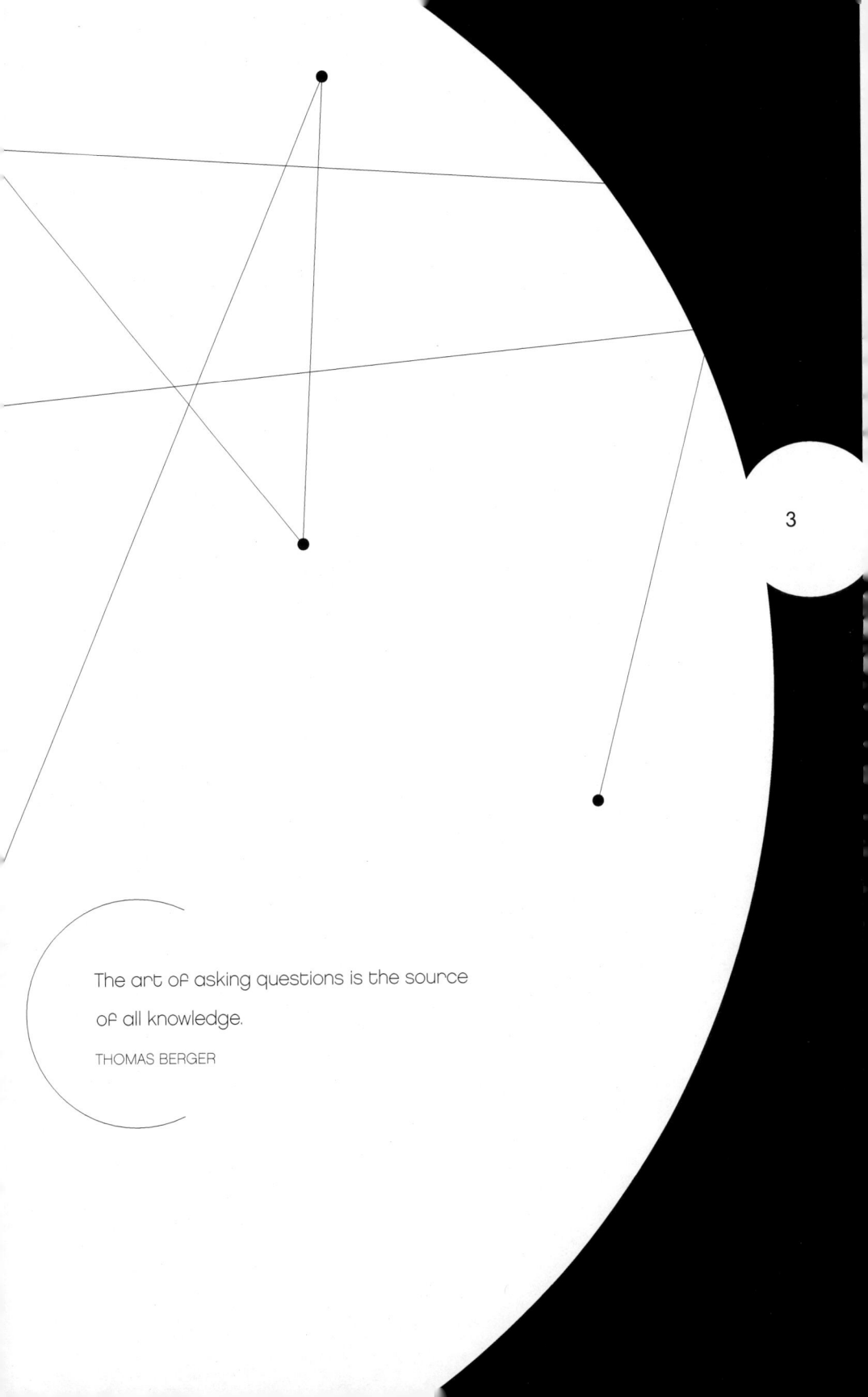

The art of asking questions is the source of all knowledge.

THOMAS BERGER

Interview with Colleen,
a choreographer

How do you define or describe clarity
as you experience it?

_____

What gets in the way of finding clarity?

_____

Why is clarity important to your work/life?

_____

What do you do to "get clear"?

_____

Simple, calm, focused. Sure (but not certain).

Indecisiveness, fatigue, disturbance.

I can proceed.

I ask myself a question.
I focus on one question at a time.

How to ask **probing** questions

It is not the answer that enlightens, but the question.

DECOUVERTES

Social activist Fran Peavey, author of "Creating a Future We Can Live With," has developed a system of strategic questioning that can be used to achieve both personal and social change. (Read her article at: http://www.context.org/ICLIB/IC40/Peavey.htm.) Designed to make a difference, a strategic question:

creates dynamic motion

creates options

digs deeper

avoids **why**

avoids **yes** or **no** answers

empowers

asks the unaskable

Not all questions are alike.

You've got your rhetorical questions, your socratic questions, and your trick questions. Then you've got your softball questions, and your leading questions. And let's not forget about the Barbara Walters designed-to-make-you-cry questions.

Like any tool, a question needs to be thoughtfully chosen and deployed in order to be effective.

An effective **probing** question encourages reflection and avoids negativity. In search of an active and creative response, it has two main characteristics. First, it is **open**-ended, rather than closed. Second, it is **neutral,** rather than judgmental.

Questions beginning with *who, when,* and *where* are generally closed queries that elicit facts rather than insight. Questions beginning with *why* can too easily imply blame.

That leaves **what** and **how.** They initiate questions that will yield the most useful information.

You will benefit most from questions like:

how did that happen?
what am I doing?
how am I feeling?
what are my choices?

The goal is to stay in the INFORMATIONAL circle, where questions are open-ended and neutral. That's where you'll mine the most valuable information about what matters most.

open   closed

neutral

How do you treat your dog?   When did you kick your dog?

informational   investigative

judgmental

How can you   How could you
treat your dog better?   kick your dog like that?

advisory   accusatory

Try this

Choose something you did recently that you want to understand better, either because you don't want to do it anymore (agree to another volunteer activity) or because you want to do it more often (have a friendly conversation with your teenager). Now write down at least five informational questions to ask yourself about that behavior.

1 _____

2 _____

3 _____

4 _____

5 _____

and then
there is a fifth
kind of question—
the musical question

How Do You Solve a Problem Like Maria?

What's It All About, Alfie?

Who Let the Dogs Out?

Where Have All the Flowers Gone?

How Much Is That Doggie in the Window?

What's Love Got to Do with It?

Who's Afraid of the Big Bad Wolf?

What Becomes of the Brokenhearted?

Why Do Fools Fall in Love?

What's New Pussycat?

> Judge others by their questions
> rather than by their answers.
>
> VOLTAIRE

ye shall know them by their **questions**

My coaching clients have proven to me time and time again that, when you yearn to live clearly and purposefully, the right questions will appear, and they will lead the way.

Take Fran, for example. Fran is a visual artist, and she was feeling profoundly aimless, despite success in both her professional and personal life. She didn't know how she wanted her artistic life to proceed, and she was dissatisfied with her day job. When she found herself nearing the end of a leave of absence, she decided it was important to have a plan in hand before she returned to work.

Fran was extremely intelligent, and articulate. On one level she had a good grasp of her situation. But it quickly became apparent that she had a major blind spot. Because she was so well-armed intellectually, it would be a challenge for her to embrace that missing piece of the puzzle. I could see immediately, she resisted going where she didn't want to go.

During our first conversation, Fran explained how hard it was for her to just hang out, without accomplishing anything. It was "scary" and "painful" for her.

I inquired further, and she elaborated. But eventually, she backpedaled. "It's not like I'm always doing something," she defended herself. "I meditate, I do yoga, and I write."

I paused to formulate a probing question, but Fran, it turned out, beat me to the punch.

"But you know, now I'm wondering. Maybe that's busy work?"

The important thing

is not to stop

questioning

Albert Einstein

ask **more**
Questions

4

it gets harder
before you get clearer

Clarity comes with courage. When the belly is calm, free of fear, the head can be clear.

BILL T. JONES

Some questions are more difficult to pose than others. The hardest questions are the ones that cut closest to the bone. These are the heavy hitters you'll need when you meet your most stubborn resistance.

I've observed this encounter time and again with my clients. Great progress will be made, but then she hits an invisible wall. It is particularly daunting and discouraging because, although you can feel it holding you back, you can't see exactly what it is you're up against. It's near impossible to deal with the invisible.

It's not unlike the experience of the marathon runner, who inevitably "hits the wall" before finishing the race. To get past it takes heart, and courage.

At the moment when you feel the most exhausted, when you are venturing beyond your comfort zone, when the path of least resistance beckons, you need to ask the hardest questions. This most treacherous stretch of the course requires you to remain relentlessly rigorous. "I don't know" is not an option. Neither is fibbing.

THE PRICE OF CLARITY IS BRUTAL HONESTY.

When the emperor leads the procession butt-naked down Main Street, you've got to be the one who inquires as to the whereabouts of his new clothes.

once upon a time

Human beings love stories. You could argue that we are *homo fabula,* the storytelling species.

Telling our stories can be liberating. Giving voice to our experience is affirming, and potentially life-changing.

But stories can also be limiting, even stultifying. The story we tell about ourselves may have been composed by someone else, perhaps our parents. It may be only part of the whole story. It may be the only story that our culture can accommodate. (Up until recently, women have had pitiful few plots from which to choose, beyond the marriage plot. Read Carolyn Heilbrun's *Writing A Woman's Life.)*

Sometimes stories function to keep problematic emotions at bay, by packaging those feelings for painless consumption. For my money, narratives are a tad too neat to reflect real life.

That's why you want to dive deeper—to connect with the emotional current that's running beneath the seemingly calm surface of the narrative. That emotion is driving your resistance. And your story may be what is shielding that emotion, rendering it invisible.

Amelia is a brilliant writer. Our work together was extensive, and she made steady progress toward the book that had always eluded her. Yet it still wasn't happening.

Amelia is the most fiercely courageous person I've ever known. Her final breakthrough to that manuscript—and an immediate publishing contract—came when she faced down an old narrative and embraced old emotions.

First, Amelia "outed" the tacit agreement in her family. Her brother, also a writer, was the talented, accomplished one. Amelia was the flake. How could she publish a book, and take away any of his glory?

4

Second, Amelia reconnected to one of her life's defining moments. When her mom died early on, Amelia was not only brokenhearted, but she felt angry at being abandoned. But, being a good girl, she felt that it was wrong to be angry at her mom. She felt ashamed to be angry, so she stuffed it away. For all these years, she'd been stuck in that five-year-old place, she realized, remaining the devil-may-care bohemian, unable to conduct her writing career as an adult with goals and self-discipline.

Within several months, Amelia had finished her book and sent it off to a publisher, who loved it. The last time we spoke (she's doing it on her own now), she had planned a schedule for revisions, plotted a marketing plan, and begun work on another book.

who is that man **behind** the curtain?

Terry came to me for coaching to help get her home-based business off the ground. As devoted as she was to her children, she was also passionate about her new enterprise. It was something she was good at and had already put off for years.

Terry worked hard to define her mission, set goals, outline a plan, and arrange a schedule. But when push came to shove, she wasn't putting in the time to launch her business. I was stumped.

After several conversations chock-full of probing questions, Terry reached her rock-bottom conviction. Given what she had seen and experienced with her own mother, her first principle was that a woman could either be a good mom or a good professional, but you couldn't be both. No wonder she never made headway, because no way would she ever shortchange her kids.

Terry's situation is a reminder that our action— or inaction—is often governed by core beliefs that are assumed at such a deep level that they are unspoken. They remain invisible behind the curtain, like the Wizard of Oz. They limit our possibilities in a way that feels beyond our control.

When we do drill down to the depth of our limiting beliefs, then we can claim ownership of—and responsibility for—our implicit choices. We can begin to make conscious choices. In Terry's case, she could embrace her belief and choose to postpone her business until her kids are grown. Or, she might end up challenging her belief to the point where she chooses to commit the time to her start-up now. Clarity brings the commitment and action, whatever that might be. The goal is to exorcise the phantom **shouldas, gottas,** and **oughtas.**

When you find yourself up against an inexplicable **shoulda, gotta,** or **oughta,** try the

five whys exercise

Begin by stating the limiting belief. Then ask the same question five times

Why is that important?

By the fifth iteration, you will be able to assess what this belief really means to you and whether you want to keep or change it.

I gotta _____

_____

_____

Why is that important?

Because _____

_____

_____

Why is that important?

Because _____

_____

_____

Why is that important?

Because _____

_____

_____

Why is that important?

Because _____

_____

_____

Why is that important?

Because _____

_____

_____

in defense of
resistance

Here's how my computer consultant describes resistance. Brian is part computer geek and part artist, and I couldn't have painted a more vivid picture:

Resistance drags the simple answers out, beats them to a pulp, and then leaves them by the stream of consciousness to die.

(BTW, Brian's ideal of clarity is the second movement of Beethoven's Seventh.)

Resistance does do damage, there's no doubt. But I'd like to put in a word for the effective use of resistance, if I may.

Resistance does damage when we don't give it the attention it craves. Resistance is information from ourself to ourself that is too important to be silenced. The more we struggle to ignore it, the more creative and noisy it gets in demand of acknowledgment.

So, instead of stuffing away your resistance, take it out into the light of day where you can keep track of it. Make friends with it. Accept and honor it, because it is a part of your being until the day you die. Actively manage it, because you don't want it to undermine your ambitions.

When we refuse to connect with our resistance, we give it power over us. That's why Lance Armstrong initiated a conversation with his cancer. That's why I ask my clients, once they've named their resistance, what do they want to say to it?

I have finally made peace with my own resistance to writing. I will never be that paragon of self-discipline who gets up every day at five in the morning to write for hours on end. I will always live with dueling desires, one to write, and the other to be a lazy bum enjoying the good life. There's "Oprah," and there's *Vogue,* and there's the garden. Who wouldn't want to wander away from the blank screen? So I don't fight it anymore. In fact,

I seek its counsel. It tells me when I need to take a break and clear my head before tackling the next page. You remember what happened to all-work-and-no-play Jack in "The Shining," don't you?

About a decade back, I encountered serious writer's block. I was beginning work on a particularly challenging and long-term project, and I felt completely and utterly exhausted by the prospect. I didn't even want to write my morning pages (more about them in the next chapter). The resistance was so overwhelming that I had to relent. "Okay," I literally told myself, "if I don't want to write, then I won't write." For the better part of a year I happily did everything but write. Then, one day, I found myself excited about the project again, figured out how it needed to be approached, and got on with it. Not writing and not thinking about writing and not obsessing about not writing was exactly what I needed to do. All because I respected the resistance.

All resistance is the same, but each person creates resistance in his own unique way.

Ask yourself

What are my particular habits of resistance?

1 _____

2 _____

3 _____

How can I get to know each one better?

1 _____

2 _____

3 _____

fear
the final **frontier**

Openness doesn't come from resisting our fears
but from getting to know them well.

PEMA CHÖDRÖN

When you find the outermost thresholds
of pain, or fear, or uncertainty, what you
experience afterward is an expansive feeling,
a widening of your capabilities.

LANCE ARMSTRONG

Fear is the most ingenious resistance of them all. It is the most debilitating, and it is the most exhilarating.

Fear plants the question: "What if . . . ?" This is endless territory where you can roam forever. Don't get sucked in. You're the one who should be asking the questions.

Instead, take a page from Susan Jeffers' classic, *Feel the Fear and Do It Anyway.*

Jeffers wants you to accept fear as a fact of life: stop trying to conquer it, and learn to live with it. "Whenever we take a chance and enter unfamiliar territory or put ourselves into the world in a new way, we experience fear. Very often this fear keeps us from moving ahead with our lives. The trick is to FEEL THE FEAR AND DO IT ANYWAY."

Jeffers breaks it down: At the bottom of every external fear ("I'm afraid of taking the wrong job") is the internal fear that you won't be able to handle something gone wrong. That's the terror that really keeps you stuck. But if you trust your ability to handle whatever happens, then fear loses the power to stymie your growth. You move from pain to power.

In fact, fear isn't a red light. Fear yells, "Do it!" Feel the fear, do it anyway, and the payoff is a more expansive life. I can personally assure you: you need only taste this exhilaration once, and you'll never again be satisfied with playing it safe.

Life shrinks or expands

in proportion

to one's courage.

Anaïs Nin

let go of what
doesn't matter
every day
in every way

I offer you one more question. It is the ultimate question.

So what?

This line comes with requisite stage directions:

So what? she laughed, with a playful shrug of the shoulders and a slight lift of the brow.

Most of the stuff that gets our knickers in a twist isn't really that important. It isn't worth squandering your time, attention, and energy.

And yet we let ourselves be distracted by minor annoyances. It gets to be habitual. Once we get sucked in by one irritation, it's easy to get sucked in by the next one, and the one after. That negative energy feeds on itself.

So what? interrupts that downward spiral. **So what?** nips it in the bud. **So what?** performed with the requisite stage directions keeps you in a lighthearted place. From there you can quickly assess the situation. Ninety-nine times out of 100, it's not worth the torment.

When the dog bites, when the bee stings, remember to ask the question.

So what?

4

Write it

down

everything
I **know**
about writing clearly
I learned
from Mrs. Parker

Never sacrifice clarity, accuracy, meaning,

for writing which sounds

good, intelligent, knowledgeable.

Remember that the purpose of language

is to convey/reveal truth,

not to obfuscate or confuse.

When I got to university, they placed me in Honor's English with Mrs. Parker. For our first assignment I pulled out all the stops. The essay was dense with the fancy syntax and thesaurus vocabulary for which I had been rewarded in high school. Imagine my surprise when Mrs. Parker chose my paper to display to the class on the overhead projector as an example of how NOT to.

What Mrs. Parker wrote at the end of that paper resounds in everything I've done since then, as a writer, educator, and now as a coach.

it's like they say, put it in writing

Muddiness is not merely a disturber of prose, it is also a destroyer of life, of hope: death on the highway caused by a badly worded road sign, heartbreak among lovers caused by a misplaced phrase in a well-intentioned letter, anguish of a traveler expecting to be met at a railroad station and not being met because of a slipshod telegram. Think of the tragedies that are rooted in ambiguity, and be clear!

STRUNK and WHITE

Writing is a further way of inquiring into yourself.

Questions yield the mother lode of raw data, but writing captures an even finer grain of information. And questions take you only so far in making sense of the answers. Writing is the way you process all that raw material. As Lauren, an HR specialist, put it, all she needs to get clear is a half hour with a pencil and paper.

Writing can serve two purposes in your quest for clarity.

First, you can use writing to **ACCESS** your intuition by journaling and freewriting.

Second, you can use writing to **COMMIT** to your intentions.

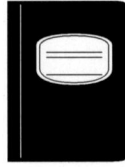

i'm writing pages in the morning

When I catch myself feeling (and acting) grumpy, I stop and ask, "What's happening?" Nine times out of ten I come to the same conclusion: I've neglected my morning pages.

Creativity guru Julia Cameron made morning pages famous in *The Artist's Way.* They are a form of journaling, the one I find most useful because it is completely unstructured. What Cameron describes as "an apparently pointless process" has been a part of my clarity practice for more than a decade.

Explore other ways to journal

The Story of Your Life
Dan Wakefield

At a Journal Workshop
Ira Progoff

Visioning
Lucia Capacchione

Cameron's instructions for morning pages are plain to understand.

Put simply, the morning pages are three pages of longhand writing, strictly stream-of-consciousness: "Oh, god, another morning. I have NOTHING to say. I need to wash the curtains. Did I get my laundry yesterday? Blah, blah, blah . . . " They might also, more ingloriously, be called **brain drain,** since that is one of their main functions.

There is no wrong way to do morning pages. These daily morning meanderings are not meant to be **art.** Or even **writing.** [. . .] Pages are meant to be, simply, the act of moving the hand across the page and writing down **whatever** comes to mind. Nothing is too petty, too silly, too stupid, or too weird to be included.

My own pages get pretty petty, pretty silly, and pretty stupid, not to mention pretty weird. I use the empty space at the top of my journal (a standard-issue Mead composition book) to record the new to-do items that come crushing into consciousness. Personally, I re-read the pages only when I've used them to work out project ideas. Otherwise, they're compost.

With morning pages I can let loose and let go of the stuff that would otherwise keep me distracted or stuck. What slips past my **So what?** during the day gets purged in my morning pages.

as the hand moves, so moves the **heart**

My other favorite writing technique is Natalie Goldberg's timed exercise (aka freewriting), popularized by her how-to classic, *Writing Down the Bones.* When I need to dig deeper, this is the tool I choose.

The goal is to capture the energy of first thoughts, unedited and uninhibited.

To do that, set a kitchen timer for ten or fifteen minutes or longer, give yourself a prompt (an open-ended topic or question), and write non-stop until the timer starts clanging. Like morning pages, freewriting is not about creating literature. It's about discovering what you don't know you know.

Goldberg specifies six rules for the timed exercise:

1. keep your hand moving

2. don't cross out

3. don't worry about spelling, punctuation, grammar

4. lose control

5. don't think

6. go for the jugular

You can use and re-use these prompts
to freewrite about a specific issue
or about life in general. Try one now.

what's happening

what's missing

what's wrong

what's working

what's next

what's best

_____

_____

5

_____

_____

_____

I have found that when I am writing something emotional, I must write it
the first time directly with hand on paper. Handwriting is more connected
to the movement of the heart.

NATALIE GOLDBERG

contract with yourself to accomplish what **matters** most

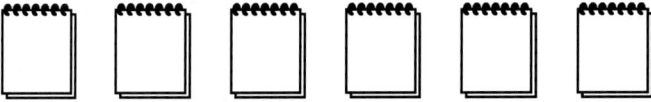

Ah, but a man's reach should exceed his grasp,

Or what's a heaven for?

ROBERT BROWNING

How could we get anything done without our lists? Grocery lists, errand lists, the mega-to-do lists called project management.

LISTS aren't just reminders, they are COMMITMENTS. I want to do it, therefore I write it down.

Our goals—whether it's the corner office or a clean car—are given a concrete reality when we set them in black and white. The very act of writing or typing the words deepens our imaginative engagement with those goals. It helps us to rehearse our ambitions.

So why don't we use lists to declare our life's desires, in addition to our favorite breakfast cereal?

I first learned about the power of the life list in college, when I visited my older brother, a med student, in Washington, DC. He lived in a big old house near Dupont Circle with a dozen other med students. His bedroom was way upstairs, in a snug, peak-roofed space. Tacked up by the telephone was a list, handwritten in his baroque-style script. I noticed it wasn't a phone number list, and I was curious. It turned out to be a list of outdoor activities, and some of them had been crossed through. I realized then how important it was for my brother to get out into nature, and to this day he hikes and fishes around the country on his weeks off from the ER.

LISTS aren't just commitments, they are CONTRACTS. I promise to do it, therefore I write it down.

By writing down what you want to accomplish, you hold yourself accountable, as if you had signed a contract. Once it's down on the page, a statement to the world, you'll find more courage and less chance to renege.

My father was fond of saying that nothing happens unless it has a budget and a deadline. True enough. But even before the budget and the deadline, you need to put it in writing: **What do you want to accomplish?**

Choose one area of your life (work, family, money, romance, education, self-care, fun, spirituality, creativity) that is currently your highest priority. Write down three things you want to accomplish in that area in the upcoming year.

1 _____

_____

_____

2 _____

_____

_____

3 _____

_____

_____

clarity is the **antidote** to a clichéd life

For George Orwell, clarity was a weapon of freedom.

In 1946, in the aftermath of World War II, the British author (*Animal Farm* and *1984*) wrote an essay entitled "Politics and the English Language." His remedy for the miserable state of the world was precise, fresh, scrupulous writing. Only this kind of clear language, born of clear thinking, would give lie to the double-speak of corrupt politicians and policies.

I read Orwell's essay as a manifesto on clarity.

Clarity is the tool that keeps language true to real meaning, rather than a hostage to empty rhetoric. Clarity prevents us from writing—or living—thoughtlessly, in readymade clichés.

CLARITY PROTECTS US FROM THE TYRANNY OF BAD HABITS.

Orwell offered four questions to keep writers honest. With a little modification, those same four questions provide the antidote to a clichéd life. If you want to accomplish what matters most, then get clear about what that means to you.

What am I trying to accomplish?

_____

_____

What thoughts, feelings, and actions will achieve it?

_____

_____

What strategy will work best?

_____

_____

Is this strategy focused enough to be effective?

_____

_____

Clarity, clarity, surely clarity is the most beautiful

thing in the world,

A limited, limiting clarity

I have not and never did have any motive of poetry

But to achieve clarity

George Oppen

acknowledgments

I owe my gratitude to many people, whose help came to me both directly and indirectly, recently and formatively.

To Angela Rodgers, for giving visual life to my words.

To my father, for teaching me the joy of file folders.

To Mrs. Parker, for teaching me the purpose of writing.

To Susan Post, for sharing her expertise on books and bookselling.

To Lorraine Daly, George Russell, Susan Tsu, Kathy Voges, Nicole Plett, Jody Wright, and LaDair Wright, for providing generous and indispensable counsel.

To my friends and colleagues, for answering questions about their experiences of clarity. To protect their privacy, I have used pseudonyms when quoting them.

To my coaching clients, for trusting me with their ambitions. To protect their privacy, I have used pseudonyms and modified descriptive details when recounting their stories.

To Ross Baldick, for giving lift to my dreams.

Get Clear and Get Going!

In this dynamic **keynote speech,** Dr. Ann Daly explores clarity not as a flash that comes out of the blue, but as a habit of mind that you can depend upon every day. Known for her passionate and incisive delivery, she engages audiences with interactive dialogue, personal stories, and dynamic slide imagery.

Discover how to harness the power of clarity to accomplish what matters most. Learn the five steps to clarity, the right questions to ask, how to handle resistance, strategies for deepening self-awareness, and the best journaling tools. With clarity comes ease and confidence in decision-making and planning. You'll focus on what's important, and commit to action.

How do audiences respond? "When attendees say the experience was 'truly outstanding' and 'potentially life-changing,' you know you have a winner."

To learn more: **keynote@anndaly.com**

Dr. Ann Daly will help you get clear about what you want and how to get it. Weekly telephone sessions will enable you to sort things out calmly, even playfully.

We will undertake a personalized conversation that is safe and confidential. Using the techniques of strategic inquiry, deep dialogue, and visualization, I will help you to see your situation clearly, identify your deepest desires, and choose your best options. You'll get there by:

expanding your field of vision
uncovering blind spots
increasing focus
shifting perspective
sharpening your eye for detail

I am so grateful for finding Ann! She is an attentive and empathetic listener, an insightful and kind teacher, and a compassionately fierce truth-teller. — Annie L.

Ann combines respect for dreams with pragmatic solutions to make them come true, one sane step at a time. — Saundra G.

Thank you so much for your quick and patient intellect, and its direction toward my needs. Your heart, too, is much appreciated. — David R.

Ann helped me to push the envelope further, stretching in new ways, in order to find the place I wanted. — Nancy J.

To learn more: **anndaly@anndaly.com**

Life Coaching

about the designer

Angela Rodgers heads the Graphic Design Program at St. Edward's University in Austin, Texas.

Rodgers co-authored "Carolee Schneemann: A Life Drawing" (2001) and *When Writing Becomes Gesture* (2004) with Ann Daly.

As a researcher, she explores visual communication that crosses cultures. She utilizes a design method that engages people to question their automatic interpretations and become aware of the structures that shape meaning. As an example, Angela Rodgers exhibited "the silk road 8* Impressions," in the SEU Fine Art Gallery in Austin based on her research and travel in China.

As a designer, she specializes in books, information, and printed ephemera.

For more information, contact Angela Rodgers at: angelasrodgers@gmail.com

about the author

Ann Daly, PhD, is a life coach, author, and speaker based in Austin, Texas. She helps women and creative professionals get clear about what they want and how to get it.

After 17 years as a university professor, Dr. Daly left to establish her own life coaching practice. Her keynotes and workshops, including "Get Clear and Get Going!," are given nationally and internationally.

Dr. Daly is the award-winning author of three books on women and the arts. She has written for the *New York Times* and *Village Voice,* and her commentary has been aired on NPR's "Marketplace."

Her work on clarity and creativity has been featured on "The Coaching Show" and in the *Australian Financial Review.*

She is the "Transitions" coaching columnist for *Your Address* magazine, and she hosts "BookWisdom," a book salon that inspires and improves women's lives.

For information about coaching and speaking services:

Ann Daly, PhD

512/454–0531

www.anndaly.com

anndaly@anndaly.com

Do you want to learn more about accomplishing what matters most? Sign up for "Get Clear," Dr. Daly's free monthly eletter, at: www.anndaly.com.